ST. JOSEPH'S UNIVERSITY   STX

LB2831.92.W44
Principals, what they do and who they ar

3 9353 00066 5479

PRINCIPALS

What They Do
and
Who They Are

by

Gilbert R. Weldy

LB
2831.92
.W44

177473

Copyright 1979

The National Association of Secondary School Principals
1904 Association Dr., Reston, Va. 22091

ISBN 0-88210-097-1

Contents

Foreword

SECONDARY SCHOOL PRINCIPALS as educational leaders are frequently called upon to meet and work with many citizens who represent a variety of community interests. These people know from their own school-day experiences that the person in charge of a school is called the principal, but unfortunately that is the extent of their knowledge about the position and the person who occupies it.

Recognizing this situation, NASSP asked Gilbert R. Weldy, a career principal for many years, to prepare this monograph not so much for other principals to read but to pass on to members of the public who seek information about *principals, what they do and who they are.*

We commend it, therefore, not just to our administrators but to all persons interested in knowing more about these leaders and the schools they serve.

Owen B. Kiernan
Executive Director
NASSP

Preface

MANY STUDENTS, PARENTS, and non-educators have only a very vague idea about what school principals actually do. They perceive principals as authority figures, educational experts, community leaders, school managers, problem solvers, and decision makers. They know the title, the position, and even the location of the office. They see the principal in and about the school and at all extracurricular activities, but many still feel unsure about what the principal does on a day-to-day basis.

Some principals doubtlessly have become discouraged and despairing of the unreasonable demands made upon them. They may feel that they do not control their jobs, that the forces outside the school pull and tug at their autonomy, making their position intolerable. They are buffeted about by student militancy, parent pressures, governing boards' interference, superintendents' influence, and legislative blundering.

All this may suggest that today's principalship is an impossible role, that principals—as suggested in a weekly news magazine—are "burned out."

This monograph is intended to dispel these doubts and uncertainties about the role of the principal and to describe and illustrate how many secondary school principals are in reality masters of their jobs, leaders in their schools, and a positive force for good education in their communities and in the country. This monograph will help parents, students, and lay persons understand more clearly the expectations, the responsibilities, and the day-to-day activities of the school principal.

Since the author is a high school principal of some 20 years experience, the descriptions throughout this monograph will be primarily of the secondary school principal (junior, middle, and senior high schools). Many of the role expectations, however, are the same for elementary principals as well. The principal's role expectations have undergone radical and significant changes in recent years. With teacher militancy, tight budgets, student activism, declining test scores, declining enrollments, and a new effort to hold school administrators accountable for their schools, principals themselves have experienced some ambivalence and uncertainty about what their role should be.

The principal of the school is seen by most people as the most important, most influential, and most powerful person in the school. His role does make a difference. The Maryland State Department of Education concluded in a 1978 study of schools whose students were high achievers on standardized tests that this achievement may be directly related to the daily performance of the school principal. The study indicated that schools with principals who have very high expectations of themselves, their teachers, and their students dominate the upper end of the test scale. They reported that much of the difference in feeling or sense of direction in the school's instructional program is attributable to the principal's leadership role.

Lest readers conclude that this monograph is self-serving—that principals want students, parents, and community members to know how important they are—here are a few additional perceptions of people outside the principalship.

In a 1977 *Chicago Daily News* series featuring six successful principals in the Chicago area, the articles were entitled "The School Principal—A Basic Key."

The articles quote Dr. William Nault, editorial director of Field Enterprises, who said, "I have rarely seen a good school without a good principal. My experience has been that the principal is really a critical factor in the excellence of a school, particularly in the instructional program of the school."[1]

Dr. Benjamin Bloom, professor of education at the University of Chicago, concurred and added, "So many principals could be running a small hospital or a small post office. But education is a special care. The problem is to get a professional leader."[2]

Dr. James Bryant Conant, who made major studies of the nation's schools and whose published recommendations have had nationwide influence, wrote, "The difference between a good school and a poor school is often the difference between a good and poor principal."[3]

Rev. Jesse L. Jackson, head of Operation P.U.S.H. (People United to Save Humanity) in Chicago, has been working closely with schools in some of our large cities to help students develop better attitudes, motivation, and study habits. He wants parents involved in more constructive and influential ways. Using the metaphor of the recipe for good education, he has said of the school principal: "The key to the educational cookie is the principal. Without his guidance and involvement, there's no telling, whether the cookie's going to come out lumpy and un-cooked or burned to a crisp.

"And unless someone—boards of education, parents, students, teachers, the community, personal pride and conscience—holds the principal accountable for making things come out right, don't ever expect any gourmet treats. The principal is the motivational yeast; how high the students and teachers rise to their challenge is the principal's responsibility. And until more principals accept

---

1. "The School Principal—A Basic Key," *Chicago Daily News*, 14 September 1977.
2. *Ibid.*
3. James Bryant Conant, *Education in the Junior High School Years* (Princeton, N.J.: Testing Service, 1960), p. 37.

their responsibility—or are made to, or are replaced—the educational cookie will continue to crumble."[4]

In a comprehensive study of school violence utilizing 5,578 schools, the U.S. Department of Health, Education, and Welfare concluded that the principal's leadership seemed to be one of the strongest factors in reducing school violence. Specifically, the study cited the principal's visibility and availability to students and staff as making the greatest difference. Schools with the least violence had principals who were educational leaders and who were behavioral role models, leading the schools by personal example. These principals were not arbitrary in siding with either students or teachers in settling disputes. They expressed "unusual strength of character" according to the HEW study, released in January 1978.

The principalship *is* one of the most critically important positions in education. This monograph is intended to help students, parents, and lay persons understand the principal's role and know what to expect of their principal.

To relieve any concern some readers may have for the author's referring to the principal by the masculine pronouns which will be used throughout this monograph, justification comes from the traditional acceptance of the masculine pronouns (he, him, his) to represent both sexes. There *are* female principals, but the great majority are male. According to NASSP's 1978 study of the high school principalship, which will be referred to frequently in this monograph, the number of female principals is only about seven percent of the total number.

—G.W.

---

4. Jesse Jackson, "The Principal Is the Key to Education," *Cincinnati Inquirer*, January 1978.

PRINCIPALS

What They Do
and
Who They Are

1

Everything to Everybody

THE IMPRESSION that many students, parents, and non-educators have of the principal and the role of this chief school administrator is that he is everything to everybody. His responsibilities are so extensive, and his influence so far-reaching, that many patrons of the school view him as the key person for getting most everything done. The fact is that the principal who is truly in charge of his school and in touch with all its dimensions, its activities, and programs *will* be able to know and do what no one else in the school can.

In 1974, the Select Committee on Equal Educational Opportunity of the United States Senate issued a report on the role of the school principal which supports this point of view:

> In many ways the school principal is the most important and influential individual in any school. He is the person responsible for all the activities that occur in and around the school building. It is his leadership that sets the tone of the school, the climate for learning, the level of professionalism and morale of teachers, and the degree of concern for what students may or may not become. He is the main link between the school and the community, and the way he performs in that capacity largely determines the attitudes of students and parents about the school. If a school is a vibrant, innovative,

1

child-centered place, if it has a reputation for excellence in teaching, if students are performing to the best of their ability, one can almost always point to the principal's leadership as the key to success.

The principal who alone tries to fulfill these many roles and responsibilities may find them insurmountable. The principal who wants to keep his thumb on every activity, every decision, every problem, every innovation, will soon give up in despair. Most principals have learned the skill of administering a complex organization like the school, and have organized, assigned, delegated, and scheduled the work to be done. They have divided it among associates, assistants, aides, secretaries, department chairmen, teachers, committees, advisory groups, and policy-making bodies. The wise principal uses all the help he can mobilze and control.

The position, then, may very well be more accurately called "the principalship," because the work is accomlished by many who assist, and not by the principal alone. He controls the activities of subordinates and therefore multiplies his own output to accomplish the far-ranging responsibilities of administering and managing a school.

The scope and variety of the principal's role and responsibilities are contained in job descriptions. These descriptions vary from school to school and will be affected by the size of the school and the number of assistants and supervisors.

This is a fairly representative job description[5] for the senior high school principal in Allentown, Pa.:

TITLE: PRINCIPAL

QUALIFICATIONS: 1. A master's degree or higher, with a major in educational administration.

---

5. NASSP, *Job Descriptions for Principals and Assistant Principals— The Current Trends* (Reston, Va.: National Association of Secondary School Principals, 1976), pp. 57-58.

2. A valid state certificate to practice as a school principal.
3. At least five years successful experience as a classroom teacher.

(Such alternatives to the above qualifications as the board may find appropriate and acceptable.)

REPORTS TO: Director of Secondary Education or Director of Elementary Education

SUPERVISES: All personnel serving in assigned school (s).

JOB GOAL: By use of leadership, supervisory, and administrative skills, to manage assigned school (s) so as to promote the educational development of each student.

PERFORMANCE RESPONSIBILITIES:
1. Studies the educational needs of the neighborhood served by the school and develops plans for meeting them.
2. Exerts leadership in the adaptation of the general program of education approved for the schools to meet the peculiar needs of the community served.
3. Directs the activities of school professional and nonprofessional staff members in the performance of their duties.
4. Supervises the instructional staff in the development and implementation of curriculum and student activities.
5. Reports to appropriate central office administrative officers regarding the needs of the school

with respect to personnel, equipment, supplies, and curriculum.

6. Develops a program of public relations in order to further the community's understanding and support of the educational program in cooperation with the assistant to the superintendent for community services.
7. Administers the school's budgeted allocations.
8. Implements board policies and administative rules and regulations relating to the school.
9. Utilizes all resources of the school system and the community in developing the most effective educational program.
10. Consults regularly with and coordinates the services of the resource personnel so that all classroom teachers may receive effective assistance.
11. Establishes guides for proper student conduct and maintaining student discipline consonant with school district policies.
12. Supervises the school's teaching process.
13. Orients newly assigned staff members and assists in their development, as appropriate.
14. Attends special events held to recognize student achievement and attends school-sponsored activities, functions, and athletic events.
15. Maintains and controls the various local funds generated by student activities.
16. Cooperates with college and university officials regarding teacher training and preparation.
17. Works with various members of the central administrative staff on school problems of more than in-school import, such as transportation, special services, and the like.
18. Conducts staff meetings to keep members informed of policy changes, new programs, and the like.
19. Keeps the superintendent informed of the school's activities and problems.

20. Performs such other tasks and assumes such other responsibilities as the superintendent may from time to time assign.

TERMS OF EMPLOYMENT:	Twelve-month year with salary to be established by the board.
EVALUATION:	Performance of this job will be evaluated annually in accordance with provisions of the board's policy on evaluation of administrative personnel.

Job descriptions and lists of duties of principals are impressive, but they still may not describe exactly what a principal does. The remainder of this monograph will describe more precisely how the principal performs these duties.

Job descriptions for junior high and middle school principals are very similar, with the level of responsibility in the school hierarchy being on the same level as the high school principal. The chief differences may be in the size of the school units, junior high and middle schools usually being smaller. The high school principal is likely to have more administrative assistance.

Assistant principals traditionally are cast in a role of assisting the principal with his duties. The assistant's role commonly includes many of the day-to-day operational responsibilities such as transportation, student activities, student supervision, attendance, and discipline. Assistant principals, who in the absence of the principal take charge of the school, typically are required to have the same training and certification as principals.

2

A Typical Day

WHAT IS IT THAT PRINCIPALS DO? is often asked by students, parents, and non-educators. Their question is both sincere and legitimate.

If a principal were to neglect planning his day, he probably would find his time totally taken up in essential tasks. Teachers, parents, students, and secretaries can dominate the principal's time with requests, conferences, phone calls, and the like. Principals have no difficulty using all of their time.

One means of describing the dimensions and complexities of this role is to present a minute-by-minute account of a day in the life of a high school principal. A comprehensive, detailed time record of how one principal in a large, comprehensive high school spent his day, October 27, 1977, is included in the appendix.

The principal described the day as fairly typical, but acknowledged that he probably spent more time on the phone than usual and also that he left school earlier than customary because of a personal appointment.

The principal's log shows that he spent eight hours and 15 minutes at school. He made 28 telephone calls, 11 of which were not completed, either busy or no answer, and received five telephone calls. Most of the calls were short, consuming only 40 minutes in total.

The paper blizzard affects the principal as well as all other executives and administrators. This principal handled 40 pieces of paper and spent 98 minutes of his day with written communications.

The principal spent three hours in meetings and appointments, one for one hour and 25 minutes, one for 28 minutes, another for 30 minutes, and another for 38 minutes. Principals find that much of their work must be accomplished in meetings and conferences.

The principal engaged in conversations with 27 different persons on 33 different subjects for a total of 82 minutes of his day. He used 28 minutes giving dictation or instructions to his secretary. His movement around the building took 22 minutes. The remainder of the time was unaccounted for or unclassified.

As illustrated in the time log, principals deal with a variety of issues and are in constant demand by staff members and constituents. Principals reported in NASSP's study of the principalship (1978) that their typical work week was 56.5 hours. They reported spending their time in (1) school management, (2) personnel supervision, (3) student activities, (4) student behavior, (5) program development, (6) district office, (7) planning, (8) community activities, (9) professional development.

Principals who try to plan too much of their day, however, will be frustrated. A principal learns to live with interruptions and many unexpected crises and emergencies. Principals cannot plan for them or anticipate when they will occur; they can only be sure that such events will arise. Nevertheless, effective principals do learn to control their time and make the best possible use of this important resource.

3

Busy Person Syndrome

As NOTED in the last chapter, the image of the principal is that of a very busy person. Everyone inside and outside the school seems to sense the heavy demands that are made upon the principal's time and energy. They see his full calendar; they see his appointments waiting in the outer office; they see distressed, sometimes angry students and parents seeking consideration; they see him in meetings and at most school activities; they see him at trouble spots in and around the school. The principal who is not busy is probably neglecting his duties.

Because of the busy-person impression most principals give, many people defer to this busy-ness and actually avoid contacts and communications with the principal, thinking that his time is too valuable to deal with what they feel are their inconsequential concerns. They remind the principal of how busy he is, greeting him with such reminders as, "Have you got a minute?" or, "I know how busy you are, but . . . " or, "This will only take a minute." This can have a reverse effect, with the principal being left out and avoided on matters that really concern him and should have his attention. The "busy principal syndrome" can cause those surrounding the principal—secretary, assistants, department heads, and others—to step in to take up the slack, possibly even over-stepping authority to spare the principal from the seemingly unreasonable demands of his job.

These practices must be curtailed lest they have the effect of insulating the principal from his clientele. Overly zealous, protective secretaries, anxious to preserve their boss's time, may unknowingly be usurping prerogatives that the principal would not want them to assume. Students, parents, and patrons who want to see the principal or talk with him should not have to undergo an inquisition to explain and justify why they need to see the head of the school.

This does not mean that principals need to have an "open door" at all times. Principals should be able to reserve time for meetings, appointments, private conferences, dictation, or consultations without being interrupted. Some principals pride themselves on having an "open door" and always being available, but at the risk of being interrupted at most inopportune times. Secretaries can screen telephone calls, take messages, or record numbers if calls come when the principal *is* occupied.

Students, parents, and patrons can expect to have time with the principal for any matter that touches his responsibility. Yet students and parents are not always sure just who it is in the school they should see about their questions or concerns. The larger the school, the more difficult such communications become. Parents may not be sure whom to call about an absence, a field trip, a bus, a schedule conflict, or what time a concert begins, but they all know that the school has a principal and he or someone in his office will know. A secretary may diplomatically and courteously defer a question or a request to someone else in authority in the school. The principal himself may delegate a matter to a teacher, counselor, or assistant.

Large schools with complex organizations and mazes of officialdom have a responsibility to inform their clientele of whom to contact about what. In the author's own school, a parent publication distributed at the beginning of each year carries a list of all personnel that a parent might conceivably need to contact with name, title, telephone extension, and areas of responsibility. This publication tells parents whom to contact for attendance questions, course selections, bus routes, payment of fees, discipline policies, complaints of all kinds, curriculum or policy questions, and others. In smaller schools, of course, these questions all might properly come to the principal who may hold many of these responsibilities himself.

An effective principal will be accessible. He can't be expected to be sitting in his office just waiting to greet anyone who may happen to drop in, but his time should be available by arrangement—that is, by appointment. Making an appointment and stating the reason for the appointment virtually guarantees that an adequate amount of time will be reserved, that the principal will have information and other resource persons available, and that the conference will not be interrupted.

Parents should be able to direct questions and seek information through the principal and his office and expect to have satisfactory answers. If the principal isn't in or doesn't have a ready answer, he or his secretary should refer the question to the appropriate person or get the answer and return the information. When parents call teachers, counselors, coaches, or whomever in the school, they should be greeted warmly, treated with courtesy and accommodated with as little delay as possible.

Principals and staff members who maintain their proper role in dealing with students and parents recognize that they are dealing with "clients," the recipients of their professional services, and should provide satisfaction if at all possible. There is nothing more irritating and inexcusable than to have parents or students get the "run-around" by being sent through the channels of a large school bureaucracy. Parents, whose children are the *only* reason for schools to exist, can and should expect a good reception and prompt service when they communicate with the school.

Parents are partners with the school in providing education, and the principal should insist that all his staff accept parents as their valued allies in the education and nurture of youngsters. A parent who is made to feel that his question is unimportant, his interest in unwelcome, or his concern is misdirected may need to speak with someone in authority—most likely the principal. Parents may not have to house and board teachers as in the pioneer days, but parents *do* pay the taxes that pay teachers' and administrators' salaries. Parents elect the lay boards of education that set the philosophy and the direction for the schools. The educators are the employees and have no recourse but to carry out the will of the community of parents, as they express their will through the authority of the board of education.

4

Becoming a Principal

Just HOW DOES one become a principal? What background of personal and professional characteristics leads to the principalship? Why would a teacher want to be a principal?

The National Association of Secondary School Principals, with support from a grant from the Rockefeller Family Fund, has just concluded a study of the senior high school principalship.[6] This study updates an earlier study made by NASSP in 1965. These two studies show that there have been some interesting and surprising changes in who the principals are in 1978.

If we were to consider only the norms and not the extremes, the 1978 survey shows that high school principals today are more likely to be white males; they are older when they first assume the principalship; and they are considerably better educated than they were in the mid-1960s.

Principals are as young as 25 and as old as 65, but most of them are in their 40s. About half of all principals are first appointed after age 35.

Principals apparently have found success and satisfaction in their positions. The study found that nearly

6. David R Byrne, Susan A Hines, and Lloyd E McCleary, *The Senior High School Principalship - Volume One: The National Survey* (Reston, Va.: National Association of Secondary School Principals, 1978)

half of the principals had been principals for 10 years or more, and more than 63 percent had been in the same position for four years or more.

Principals are well-educated. Nine percent of the nation's senior high school principals hold doctorates; and 85 percent of them have formal education beyond the master's degree. In 1965 only one principal in 100 held a doctor's degree, and half reported a master's degree or less.

The "route to the principalship" has changed somewhat from 1965 to 1978. There are no predominant subject areas that have led to the principalship, but the greatest number of principals in 1965 were trained in the humanities. The natural sciences and mathematics also had a high percentage. There was a perceptible shift in 1978, when more principals indicated having training in the social sciences and the sciences. It is not true that most principals have their training in physical education (11 percent in 1965, and 17 percent in 1978), although many principals have been successful athletic coaches.

The career route in 1965 was typically from the elementary principalship or from work as guidance counselors. In 1978, the career route was more likely to be through the high school assistant principalship, the high school athletic directorship, or the junior high/middle school principalship or assistant principalship. Some principals served in more than one of these positions.

In all cases high school principals have had successful teaching experience, usually from four to 10 years. Most states require at least three years of successful teaching experience, plus a master's degree for certification as a principal.

In earning a master's degree, most principals undertake training designed to prepare them for school administration. Principals in the 1977 study named the following areas of training as the most important preparation: school management, curriculum and program development, school law, supervision of instruction, human relations, secondary school principalship, school finance and budgeting, personnel administration, leadership, community relations, child and adolescent development, psychology of learning, counseling and guidance theory and practice, and negotiations.

All these data concerning *how* principals arrive at this professional position do not explain *why*. Many principals are overwhelmed by the pressure and demands of the job, but most report that they experience a certain amount of prestige and self-fulfillment in their role. Principals become principals because they want more influence in educational decisions and planning. They enjoy leadership and believe that they have skills that would make them successful. They may even like the prestige of being the "boss" or the head person in the school. Status is important to principals.

Finally, principals are also motivated by the financial rewards, usually somewhat greater than those for teachers, although the higher salaries earned by principals are not so impressive when work day, week, and/or year are compared to the classroom teacher's. Principals are usually employed for at least 10 months, many for 11 months. In most large cities and suburban areas, principals are employed year-round with a certain number of days granted for vacation (20 days is common).

Principals throughout the country reported 1977 salaries that averaged $25,600. Principals have made some salary gains in terms of "real dollars" since 1965. Principals in schools in the Mid-Atlantic states and on the West Coast receive the highest salaries; principals in the South and Southwest, the lowest.

What are principals aiming for in their professional careers? Although few are interested in lateral movement—that is, moving from one school to another—the number of principals who aspire to the superintendency or school district positions increased substantially from 1965 to 1978 (33 percent of the principals in 1978 identified that as their goal). This is undoubtedly a reflection, at least in part, of the advanced formal training of principals, who by virtue of their training would qualify to be superintendents or central office assistants.

The person wanting to become a high school principal should expect to spend from five to 10 years in the classroom, the subject area not significantly important. During these teaching years, he should earn at least a master's degree in courses designed to prepare for secondary school administration. During the years of teaching experience the teacher should use every opportunity to get a variety of experiences in organizing, leading, and supervising school programs and activities. Coaching, directing, chairing, assuming responsibility, and showing independence and resourcefulness will help in the preparation for the principalship. Opportunities as an intern administrator, assistant principal, dean, department chairman, and director of athletics will provide solid experience for the next step—the principalship. The opportunities are fewer, but they are there for the person who has made the preparation and has the drive and motivation to seek and win the appointment.

5

Identity as a Person

STUDENTS SOMETIMES have difficulty remembering that the principal is a person—a human being who lives in a house, has a family, belongs to a church, goes shopping, visits the theater, drives a car, and does all the usual things that ordinary people do. Especially in large schools the student perception of the principal too often is of a severely countenanced person standing with arms folded and glaring at some suspicious student activity in the hallway of the school. Or he may be seen as the mysterious and unseen presence presiding in an office protected by a bank of secretaries and assistants whose mission in life seems to be to keep people away from him. Or he may be thought of as the disembodied voice that comes regularly into classrooms over the public address system—issuing orders, giving advice, and pronouncing official decrees. He is often seen by students in earnest conversation with teachers, other administrators, or with parents, apparently engaged in serious deliberations over affairs of state, certainly not open to the intrusion of ordinary students.

Consequently, the principal has an image problem that is difficult to overcome. In spite of efforts he might make to relate on a human level with students by being around their activities, attending their meetings and performances, or including them in his councils, students are likely to be somewhat in awe of the principal and what he represents—authority, position, and power. Parents may add to this perception because of their own recollections and their own experiences with principals in their school days.

So principals go about their daily activities outside the school experiencing some rather unusual social behavior from students (and parents) who just aren't expecting to see their principal in "human" situations. The reaction is always amusing—a furtive look and pointed finger, guarded whispers behind the hand, or a not-so-guarded exclamation, "Why, that's our principal!" Somehow students don't expect to see their principal riding a bicycle, buying popcorn in the theater, pushing a cart in the supermarket, attending church or temple, or lounging on a beach. Some students react with surprise when they see their principal in such worldly occupations as walking to school, mowing his lawn, painting his house, or playing ball with his children.

This "image" problem prompts some principals to question seriously whether they can and should live in their school community and have their own children attend the school where they work. In small schools located in "self-contained" communities this is expected and accepted. Most of the teachers and staff live in the community and the teachers and the principals' "kids" attend the school together. In other circumstances, principals may prefer some anonymity away from their work and may prefer to live in another community.

The principal is a public person. If he has been in a school for some while, he is known by virtually every student. He cannot walk the streets, visit a restaurant, or conduct business without being seen, recognized, and greeted—sometimes in a manner that is awkward or embarrassing to him. For example, uncomplimentary cat-calls may come from a passing car whose riders hunch down from his view.

The author remembers with some pleasure the period during the summer prior to his assuming a new position in a new community—and before he was recognized on sight by every high schooler in town—being able to go to the local pool, shop in the stores, and be about the neighborhood without being spotted and identified as "the principal."

What is described here as an image problem may not be viewed as all bad by many principals. Some may not choose to live in their own school community and may not wish to have their own children attend school where they are principals, but they do try to maintain human, personal relationships with their students. They enjoy their associations with students and appreciate having students recognize and hail them away from school. Successful principals try to help students; and parents know them as persons, not just as principals.

One such successful principal in this regard was featured in the *Chicago Daily News*.[7] He was described as the "principal who keeps in touch," one whose philosophy is to be interested in what his students are doing. The report further described him as being around his school visiting with students, finding out what they are up to, commenting on their achievements, showing them that he cares, and encouraging teachers to attend student activities to show their interest in students. The principal was quoted as saying, "I feel I get along well with the kids. After all, I got into this business many years ago because I enjoy working with kids."

Principals who enjoy students will be perceived by them as real persons. Principals will overcome the image problem by some fairly simple and obvious means. First, he will be visible to students by being around the school, in the hallways, the student cafeteria, in and out of classrooms, and of course at many of the student performances, games, and activities.

---

7. Don Wycliff, "The School Principal—A Basic Key," *Chicago Daily News*, 17 September 1977.

The principal will participate in club meetings, homerooms, awards programs, and social activities where students are involved. The principal, insofar as possible, will learn to know students by name. Nothing impresses students quite so favorably as to have someone like the principal recognize and call them by their proper names.

Above all, the activities of the principal should constantly demonstrate that he cares about students, shows interest in *them* as persons, and identifies with their successes and disappointments. By doing so, they will view *him* as a person and will relate to him as a real human being — not just as an awesome individual — known as the principal.

6

An Authority Figure

IN SPITE OF HOW FAIR, friendly, and candid a principal may be, many students and parents view him as the ultimate authority in the school. They see him not only as the head person in the school but also as the person with the power.

Students recognize the principal as the one person who can, in the end, exercise the most influence over their destiny. He can set rules for them; he can assign and schedule them; he can select and appoint them; he can detain and suspend them; in some schools he can corporally punish them; and he is the one who can expel them.

State governments have given school principals this authority in very specific legislation. Many states have actually mandated that each school unit should have a principal. They have invested in him the authority to carry out the mission of the schools. The authority to manage a school, of course, is accompanied by an equal amount of responsibility and accountability. When principals are placed in school buildings with authority, they accept the responsibility and expect to be held accountable for their performance.

The principal's authority, however, is limited. Such limits have become more and more restrictive on the principal's authority through the years, but he is nevertheless expected to hold the responsibility and is held accountable. This balance between authority and responsibility is a delicate one and repeatedly places principals in precarious positions.

Most principals would prefer not to capitalize too much on this "authority figure" image. Some might find a degree of healthy fear from students to be useful, but most would rather have respect and good will from students.

Principals who function as leaders of their faculties and who provide guidance and supervision for students do not need to rely on raw power to carry out their responsibilities. They have developed administrative techniques and leadership styles that help them win cooperation and support in the pursuit of the school's educational objectives. The authority is there if needed in a crisis or in a "show down," but most process-oriented principals do not find it advantageous to use it. In no case would they ever want to flaunt it.

Being an "authority figure" to students and parents is not a very comfortable role for many principals. It is in this area that lie some of the real-life hazards of serving as a school principal. The fairest, most open principals are still the objects of abuse and acrimony from those who are angry with the school or someone associated with it. Their anger is sometimes directed at the principal personally and other times at his property. Principals' cars and homes have been vandalized—not because of any specific action or decision—but because they are seen by spiteful, disgruntled students as the authority in the school and the only target for their anger.

In every school there are a few such students without healthy, normal inhibitions and controls who will "act out" against the school's authority figure. Such actions by unknown students are extremely difficult to understand and to accept.

The principal's greatest strength is not in raw, unfettered power, but in skillful leadership, based on knowledge, good human relations, and ability to get things done.

7

Advocate for Students

WHAT DOES A PRINCIPAL stand for? A good principal must be, first and foremost, an advocate for the students. Schools exist for students and the principal must work vigorously in the school and community for the best opportunities and programs for students. He campaigns for adequate facilities. He seeks the best equipment and supplies. He recruits and searches for the very best teachers and staff members. He pushes for the most suitable and useful curricular offerings. He develops plans, generates recommendations, and advocates the adoption of new programs and new methods that will enhance education for his students.

Students should realize, however, that what the principal advocates may not be what certain groups of students want. During the late '60s and early '70s, students in high schools all over the country were agitating for fundamental changes in the substance and structures of their education. They protested and rebelled against the authority of the school and the relevancy of their education. Many policies and programs changed as a result of these protest activities. Students and some of the their parents used the courts and legislatures to bring about changes.

Consequently, students gained more freedom and the schools lost much of their authority and control. Students were given more responsibility for their own education. They were given many options to choose from in meeting their requirements. The school day was opened at both ends, and in many schools in the middle. These trends were not all supported, let alone advocated by principals. In many schools principals resisted, but the changes rolled over them nevertheless.

Today many principals are able to see the effects of some of this permissiveness: lower academic performance, excessive absenteeism, drug abuse, and declining national test scores. As a result, many principals and parents are becoming advocates of more structure and control, more attention to basic learnings, and more discipline generally. Even at this time, some of these efforts by principals will be viewed by some students and parents as punitive or repressive, but principals have seen the failure of many of their students under the more "open" systems and are actively advocating more structure — all in the interests of the best education for young people.

In addition to being an advocate for students in general, the principal must be an advocate for students individually. Many times secondary school students are unfairly accused, inaccurately stereotyped, or even unjustly punished by someone in the school. Parents misunderstand and mishandle situations with their own children. This frequently takes the form of unreasonable expectations for high grades, inflexible rules of behavior, or conflict and competition among siblings. The principal should advise parents and intercede in behalf of students whenever he believes they have been dealt with rashly or unjustly. As the "in loco parentis" person in the school, he should protect students' welfare and their rights. In many cases he becomes an advocate for students in conflict situations.

The principal walks a very thin line in this regard because he is expected at the same time to support the teacher or staff member. Parents need his support too. His guiding principle, just as should be the case with parents, is to be the advocate for the student and defend him when he is *right*, and see that consequences for misbehavior are fair and reasonable when the student is wrong.

The principal, in behalf of students, must also constantly be an aggressive advocate for good teaching. In no other area is the principal's influence felt more than in his insistence that every teacher be well prepared every day with interesting, challenging lessons and activities. The principal should be in classrooms observing teachers, offering support and suggestions. He should have an ongoing inservice program for improvement of the instruction in the school. This advocacy of good teaching may be the most important single influence the principal can have in providing students with a school that is a comfortable, exciting, stimulating, learning place.

Beyond the school itself, the principal will be advocating the provision of appropriate resources and legal guidelines for his school to do its best for all students. These outside influences on the school are considerable and frequently seem to be beyond any one principal's control and ability to change. They include local boards of education, regional service agencies, state education offices, state legislatures, and increasingly federal government agencies. Add to these the athletic conferences, the state activities associations, and the regional accrediting agencies.

Too often these far-removed agencies, operating out of their insulated ivory towers, attempt to mandate programs and services that are of doubtful value and may produce costly interferences with the educational programs that the principal considers important in his school.

How does the principal's influence extend to all these agencies and legislative bodies? He, of course, may have individual influence, and may even have a vote in some of the bodies that legislate rules affecting students, but in most cases his influence will be a collective one through professional association with his peers. Principals who are active in their professional associations—local, state, and national—have opportunities to influence legislation, to promote sound programs, and to advocate improvements in schools. Most state principals' organizations and the National Association of Secondary School Principals maintain staffs and sponsor committees of principals who engage in legislative action. Their aim is to support legislation beneficial to students and schools and to oppose actions that would adversely affect young people.

What do principals stand for? What do principals want for their students? The NASSP national survey of the high school principalship[8] furnishes considerable insight on these questions.

Principals were asked in the survey to rank statements about the educational purposes of schools. In both the 1965 and the 1978 surveys, principals ranked first the "acquisition of basic skills (reading, writing, and computing)." In comparing the two surveys, with 13 very tumultuous years intervening, principals' values held constant. In the top four purposes, principals ranked in both surveys "development of skills and practice of critical intellectual inquiry and problem solving" and "development of moral and spiritual values." The 1978 survey found the purpose of "development of positive self-concept (and good human relations)" in second rank (seventh in the 1965 survey).

In descending order in the 1978 ranking were all the following:

5. Career planning and training in specific entry level occupational skills.
6. Knowledge about and skills in preparation for family life.
7. Understanding of the American value system (political, economic, social).
8. Preparation for a changing world.

---

8. Byrne, Hines, and McCleary, *Senior High School Principalship*, p. 45.

9. Physical fitness and training in useful leisure time sports.
10. Development of skills to operate a technological society (engineering, scientific).
11. Appreciation for and experience with the fine arts.

Principals do believe strongly in some of the fundamental values that students and parents endorse as well. They can be expected to be strong advocates for these programs in their schools.

8

Rights of Principals

PRINCIPALS HAVE BEEN BUSY in the last decade learning to recognize and respond to all of the various rights movements which have affected the schools. There has been, of course, a tremendous emphasis on students' rights, giving to students all the civil and constitutional rights enjoyed by all citizens. There have also been strong movements in civil rights, bringing about long overdue racial equality in educational opportunity. Add to these the women's rights movement which has been fully implemented in most schools through Title IX of the 1972 Education Amendments.

Of course, teacher rights have been paramount and aggressively asserted through the collective bargaining process, described more fully in the next chapter. Parents have become more aggressive in insisting on their rights as their tax bills increase and they lose confidence in the product and performance of the school.

All of these movements have been necessary and have brought reforms to education that have improved each group's influence and role. The point of all of this is to bring to the attention of students, parents, and lay persons that principals have rights too.

Principals, of course, enjoy the same civil and constitutional rights that all citizens enjoy, but the responsibilities and obligations of the principal require an interpretation of how these rights apply to the principal's situation.

These rights should be accorded to all principals, not only as basic to their human condition, but also to their needs in fulfilling the expectations that communities have for the schools.

1. The right to a specific, comprehensive job description outlining the professional duties and responsibilities that are expected in the position of principal (see Chapter 1).
2. The right to have invested in the position sufficient authority and autonomy to carry out these specified duties and responsibilities. This authority will derive from state legislatures, state departments of education, local governing boards, and the office of the local superintendent of schools.
3. The right to at least an annual comprehensive evaluation of the principal's professional performance of his duties, in all cases based on objective data and direct observation of his activities.
4. The right to an appeals process to review his evaluation if the principal has reason to disagree with the conclusions or to object to the processes employed.
5. The right to have full reason given him in the event his employing board should determine that the principal's service is unsatisfactory and demotion or dismissal is contemplated. This right should also include a process for review of such a decision and an opportunity to appeal. (These rights described in points four and five suggest ordinary due process.)
6. The right to have a prominent voice in the determination of any district-wide decisions, governing board policies, or bargained agreements that would substantially affect the principal in the performance of his duties. Particularly, the principal should have the right to select professional staff assigned to his school and also screen and

recommend people employed in other positions under his supervision.

7. The right to participate in and employ various inservice improvement programs for professional improvement and advancement. This would include membership in and attendance at the local, state, and national professional associations for principals, with expenses for membership and attendance at least partially paid for by the employing district to encourage such participation.

8. The right to adequate resources in both material and personnel to carry out the school's objectives. In larger schools, this suggests administrative assistance, properly trained specialists, and sufficient clerical and classified help. Building facilities and staff limitations frequently impinge on the principal's ability to accomplish what is expected.

9. The right to adequate compensation in salary and fringe benefits that recognize the status, responsibilities, and time demands of the principalship.

10. The right to be accorded the respect and courtesy deserving of a significant leadership position in the community.

There need not be any competition or conflict in protecting the rights of all parties involved in the school—including the school principal.

9

Person in the Middle

THE SINGLE MOST DRAMATIC development in the success and satisfaction a principal derives from his role has been the advent of teacher negotiations. No other movement in education has affected the principal so much. When teachers organized into unions or "professional associations" to bargain conditions of employment directly with their employers, boards of education, principals were caught in the middle.

Their dilemma was determining which way to turn: to ally with their teachers with whom they may have enjoyed a close professional relationship, or to ally with school boards and sit across the table from teachers while they seek better pay, more desirable teaching conditions, protection of their rights, and more influence in decision making. Principals who perceived their chief role as decision maker and supervisor saw their influence and power eroding.

During the initial experience with collective bargaining in education the question of where the principal belonged was a troublesome dilemma which swirled and boiled in every professional meeting of principals. In some states where bargaining is just beginning, principals are still trying to find a comfortable spot. They find that they are not wanted as spokesmen for the teachers. Teachers today speak for themselves and do not look to administrators to be their advocates. Their faith has been transferred from their administrators to their organization's collective strength in the classic mode of labor unions in this country.

The principal who vacillates or who tries to play both sides of the street is in a losing strategy. He will eventually be forced to side with the employer, in line with his role as the middle management representative in the school. This switch in roles has been particularly troublesome for some principals of smaller schools where the principal still views himself as a member of the faculty, retaining teacher status while assuming the duties of the principalship.

Further complicating this position for the principal is the rather common practice of tying the principal's compensation to the teachers' salary schedule on some sort of index. The teachers, when they bargain for their own salaries and fringe benefits, are in effect also bargaining for the principal. When the principal moves to the table on the side of the employer, as is frequently the case today, he sits as an adversary to teachers, whose goals he may be expected to oppose and resist.

Professional associations for school administrators such as the National Association of Secondary School Principals have clearly placed the building principal on the side of management. This clarification of role has been accepted by most teachers as they gain experience with the bargaining process. Although it may interfere seriously with the principal's ability to lead teachers, particularly during bitter bargaining and strikes, the responsibilities of school leadership are important and necessary. They can be carried out by principals who accept their new role and relationship with teachers, develop new strategies and techniques for administration, and continue to deal with teachers individually on a professional, humane level. There may not be perfect harmony, but there need not be violent discord either.

The role of the principal in a school under a negotiated contract is prescribed and delineated by the terms of the agreement. His day-to-day activities are limited and defined. Particularly in the areas of teacher rights, supervision of teachers, duties, assignments, and the definition of the work day, the principal's prerogatives are severely curtailed. He now becomes the employer's guardian of the contract provisions, the first level of appeal for teacher grievances, and the arbiter and enforcer of the board of education's contractual obligations.

In one comprehensive master contract, developed over a 12-year period of collective bargaining, the building principal is mentioned 60 times, usually in provisions that limit or prescribe his supervisory activities. Examples include:

- Length and frequency of faculty meetings.
- Length of the school day.
- The number of students that can be placed in a class.
- The number of classes and periods teachers may be assigned.
- The number of consecutive periods a teacher may be assigned.
- The number of different classrooms a teacher may be assigned.
- The teachers' non-teaching duties.
- The length of the teachers' lunch period.
- Provision of clerical assistance for teachers.
- The requirement to notify teachers before a supervisory observation.
- The length of a supervisory visit.
- The requirement to hold conferences, make "constructive" suggestions, and place in writing reports of supervisory visits.
- Elaborate and laborious steps of due process for discipline or dismissal of teachers.
- Teacher participation guaranteed in decision making on school schedules, textbook selection, school policies.

- Grievance procedures that invariably begin with the principal.
- Provision of telephone service, offices, lunch rooms, teaching equipment, and clean parking lots.

Today's principal cannot remain comfortably in the middle any longer. In states that have legislation governing public employee bargaining, the principal and others responsible for hiring, assigning, evaluating, and supervising the employee group are excluded from the "bargaining unit." Where such arrangments prevail, principals have accepted their management role and are developing the required skills and strategies for successful school administration.

Putting the principal into the management role has caused a serious strain on relationships with teachers. Following a bitter round of bargaining with the usual threats of strikes, slowdowns, and other coercive actions by the teacher group and/or the employer group, the principal is expected to preside over the uneasy truce that usually results and to bring all parties happily back together. This expectation becomes impossible, particularly when the faculty has split—some loyal to the teachers' bargaining group which may have been on strike and some loyal to their contract and to their students and remaining on the job.

The principal in such circumstances is not only in the middle, between his board of education and his teachers, but he stands as mediator and referee between the alienated factions within his own faculty.

10

An Educational Leader

P<small>RINCIPALS</small> PREFER TO DESCRIBE their function with the phrase "educational leader." It suggests importance, respect, and influence. At the same time, there probably isn't a single accepted definition of what an "educational leader" is, let alone what one does.

The principal began as head teacher or "principal" teacher. When schools of the nineteenth century were organized with more than one teacher, someone was designated as the head and was responsible for certain administrative duties (and some janitorial chores as well). As schools grew in size, as grade levels were separated, and as teachers were assigned to each grade level, the need for planning, scheduling, coordination, and supervision developed. Principals were appointed to meet this administrative requirement.

The first principals continued as teachers and retained their classroom responsibilities. The principal's relationship with other teachers was collegial, his role being that of head teacher, but not necessarily the supervisor.

As schools in cities and suburbs grew and the complexity and the extent of the school's mission expanded, the need for coordination and supervision of the school's program increased. The principalship developed to fulfill that need. The persons who have qualified for that position and have sought it are the teachers who have leadership qualities, who have earned respect, and who seek influence and status. All principals have been "successful" teachers. All states now require special certification for any educator who assumes an administrative post, including the principal, assistant principals, and department chairmen who supervise other teachers. Since the early 1900s school administration has been studied and taught as a separate area of training, calling for special knowledge and expertise. Most universities provide this training in departments of administration in their schools of education. Some specialists in training administrators consider their field a science and conduct research and study the field as any other academic discipline. Others would be more inclined to call school administration an art.

To gain administrative certification in virtually any state today, the school principal needs several years of successful teaching experience and a master's degree with required courses in school history, law, finance, administration, philosophy, supervision of instruction, research methods, curriculum, public relations, and psychology of learning.

With such training, does the principal automatically become the desired "educational leader" in his school? Not necessarily. Leadership in this context is no different from leadership in any field of endeavor. Qualities of leadership that help the principal lead his faculty and students in the pursuit of their school's objectives would be similar to those required by political, business, or industrial leaders. Most successful principals would be leaders in any profession they might have chosen.

Studies of leadership are part of the training for principals. Educational leadership by the principal is not an automatic result of his assumption of the office. Leadership, particularly in recent years, has been in the *function* of the principal, not in the status or the authority of the position. The educational leader, just as all others, must assume leadership by exhibiting qualities needed by all leaders: knowledge, initiative, consideration, fairness, energy, goal orientation, process-wisdom, organizing ability, and skill in moving and motivating. Position-power and status-authority do not produce educational leadership.

Principals may have been able to function as benevolent dictators in some past day. They may have prided themselves in mental toughness and decision-making ability, but that era has passed. Principals today need enlightened leadership skill and personal qualities to provide direction and impetus to the educational goals of their schools.

11

An Acknowledged Expert

WHAT DOES A PRINCIPAL NEED to know to be a good principal? Good principals are acknowledged experts in the field of education and more specificially in the field of administration. Because of their training, they know stages of child development, levels of learning readiness, various learning styles, and effective teaching methodology. They cannot be expert in every subject area, but they can and should be experts in the teaching and learning processes. A junior high school principal featured in the *Chicago Daily News* story on school principals in September 1977, described his role as a "teacher of teachers" and said, "I try to motivate teachers to do the best job they can. And I try to get them to stretch and do some things they maybe didn't think they could do."

One of the primary responsibilities of a principal is supervising the faculty. He observes teaching in his school regularly to be intimately aware of what kind of teaching is going on; he knows the strengths, the weaknesses, the styles, the idiosyncracies of his staff. In observing teachers, the principal has the responsibility to compliment the accomplished, support the inexperienced, counsel with the specialists, and correct or eliminate the incompetent. In his role as supervisor of the instructional program the principal is a skilled observer, evaluator, and adviser to teachers.

In addition to the direct observation of classroom instruction, the principal improves instruction by providing inservice programs and by using every means available to help keep teachers current in their fields of study and familiar with the best teaching materials and equipment. He should encourage participation by his faculty in various professional activities. The publications, the conventions, and the research by professional organizations can keep teachers updated, involved, and contributing in their field. Good principals plan and carry out inservice improvement programs for teachers by utilizing outside speakers, films, resource persons, and by conducting faculty meetings, workshops, and institutes.

Possibly of most importance is the role of the principal in motivating the faculty, of stimulating, inspiring, sometimes prodding them to reach the goal of being well-prepared, enthusiastic, skillful teachers in every class every day.

Principals also need to know school law. It is simply not enough today to know the state school code on attendance requirements, mandated areas of study, teacher certification, and the required school calendar. The school principal also needs to be familiar with civil law as it applies to students in school.

In the last 15 years, the United States Constitution has been applied in many areas of school authority and discipline. These are areas in which principals at one time exercised their own discretion and judgment. Principals now must be certain that their students' First Amendment rights are protected. They no longer can exercise absolute control of student expression, petitioning, and publications. School dress is no longer the responsibility of the school to regulate, nor is the length or style of students' hair. The famous *Tinker* case in Iowa reached the U.S. Supreme Court in 1969, and settled the issue of freedom of speech by school students. It guarantees that students may exercise "symbolic" speech by wearing buttons and insignia. They may express their opinions, petition, and distribute literature even though it may be unpopular or critical of the school. The only limitation is that the "educational process" not be disrupted by students exercising this right. The principal may not prevent the exercise of this right unless he has clear and present evidence that the expression would substantially disrupt the order in the school.

Students also have been guaranteed their rights of due process, just as any citizen outside the school. Principals must know how to set up and conduct hearings and preside over appeals and to render fair, impartial judgments.

Federal laws and court decisions have opened a whole new area of knowledge needed by principals as the federal influence and funds have reached into the schools. Most of the federal programs available are useful and helpful, but they are accepted at a price—applications to prepare, forms to fill out, regulations to follow, and reports to file—many of them under the principal's direction.

In addition to the knowledge of school law, the principal stands as the school's official representative in important voluntary associations as well. Most schools belong to regional accrediting associations which assure schools and colleges and their constituents that the school is maintaining at least minimal standards of quality (and quantity). These standards are comprehensive, covering every phase of the school program: teacher, counselor, specialist, administrator qualifications; student-teacher ratio; buildings and equipment; library facilities and services; number of courses offered in every subject area; per-pupil expenditures; special education programs; and a myriad of other qualitative and quantitative standards.

The principal is expected to know these standards and to be sure that they are maintained in his school. He should also participate in the deliberations of the accrediting association by serving as the school's official representative to the annual meeting, voting in the referenda, filing the annual report, and assisting in programs of research and service.

The accrediting associations, in addition to setting minimum standards for their members, also require periodic self-evaluations which usually involve a year to a year-and-a-half of committee work by the faculty, surveying and studying every aspect of the school. The self evaluation is followed by a visit from a committee of educators from other schools and colleges who spend three to four days in the school to provide advice and counsel. All of this evaluation activity is under the direction of the principal. He is also expected to serve on visiting committees in other schools.

The North Central Association of Schools, the largest (19 states) of the voluntary accrediting groups, offers membership to elementary, junior highs, and middle schools in addition to senior high schools, and has policies and standards for all kinds of special purpose schools (college preparatory, vocational, and adult) as well as comprehensive schools. The principal will have close knowledge of all accrediting provisions and keep his school in conformance if he expects other schools and colleges to accept his students' credits and credentials on the official transcripts of records.

In addition to belonging to the voluntary accrediting associations, most schools are also members of state activities associations which sponsor and supervise interscholastic competition, both athletic and non-athletic (speech, music, academic). Again the principal is the school's representative in these associations to keep his school's activity program in compliance with all rules and regulations governing contests; eligibility, season limits, coaching qualifications, number of contests, contest supervision, state tournament series, and financial accountability. The principal ensures that his school remains in good standing and follows all the rules, or his athletic teams may be disqualified or forfeit contests.

The requirements of membership in state activities associations are becoming more complex and burdensome for the principal, particularly with the rapid expansion of girls' sports activities. The principal who neglects this responsibility can be in serious difficulty.

Although a principal cannot have specific knowledge of every curricular area taught in his school, his knowledge should at least embrace the general trends and movements within each subject area. He must have sufficient knowledge to understand and evaluate curricular innovations that are being tried in schools throughout the country. Some may be sound improvements developed under careful professional supervison. Others may be narrow opinions by self-interest groups, while still others may be gimmicks and would have no value. The principal needs the knowledge and the ability to perceive the difference.

The principal needs to determine whether an idea is worthy or not and whether it will be useful in his school. In making this decision, of course, he will need the advice of the curriculum experts in each subject area, his teachers and their immediate subject area supervisors.

Some of the "innovations" which swept the country during the late '60s and early '70s have proved ineffective and counterproductive for many students. Open campus, pass-fail grading, optional exams, and uncontrolled elective systems are examples.

Possibly the most critical area in which principals need to have expertise is human relations. The many conflicting forces, legal restraints, and special interests have been described in other parts of this monograph. The principal will have the skill and the personal attributes to moderate all these influences and bring people together to work in harmony. This talent is not taught but is absolutely essential for the successul principal today. He will be able to accept feelings, resolve differences, reach compromises, and keep all parties unified in working together toward the school's stated objectives. This requires knowledge of human psychology, group processes, and effective communication.

Parents, students, and community patrons should be able to expect their school principal to be the education expert in the school.

12

A Decision Maker

PRINCIPALS TRADITIONALLY have prided themselves in being able to make decisions—especially tough ones. This was especially true when principals saw themselves as the titular heads of their schools, invested with considerable power, and able to decide the destiny of anyone or everyone associated with the school. During that era the decision, not the process, was important. The decisions were seldom challenged, sometimes not even explained. Principals were admired for "running" good schools. Their authority was virtually absolute. It included hiring and firing teachers, making curriculum plans, organizing the school day, making teacher assignments, and, of course, punishing students who misbehaved.

Fortunately times have changed in this aspect of the principals' responsibilities. Today's principals are very process oriented and their decisions are unquestionably more difficult. One principal of a large highly organized school was asked what decisions he had made recently, and he acknowledged that he could not think of one that he had made himself without first consulting and advising with those who might share responsibility with him or who might be affected by the decision.

This expectation of teachers, students, parents, and lay people that they will have some input into decisions that affect them has confused and frustrated many principals. The process never seems "right" to all those affected. The old saw that "if the process is right, the decision will be right" just doesn't hold up any longer.

The frustration principals feel with this process-oriented age in which they now work was well-demonstrated in a survey conducted by the author several years ago, when he asked 40 suburban high school principals to identify their greatest "time wasters." Among the 10 greatest time wasters were these: conflict resolution, over-involvement of too many people, and elaborate appeals procedures. This would indicate that principals have set up procedures to involve all their publics in their administrative decisions, but that the time consumed seems to be excessive and not particularly helpful in smoothing the way to well-accepted decisions.

Making a sound, acceptable decision in any area of school life can become extremely complicated. A principal who wants to make an important change may find himself embroiled in controversy, trying to set up committees, hearings, and appeals so that everyone who wants a piece of the decision has a fair chance. Areas of decision making which are particularly troublesome and which have placed principals in unholy tugs-of-war with constituents have usually been curriculum, grading, ability grouping, the school schedule, integration, student discipline, and selection of administrators and supervisors. These are issues that have never been totally and finally settled—and probably never will be.

How might a principal expect to involve his constituents in a decision, for example, to change the format of the school's daily schedule? Teachers will expect to have a voice in that decision. It will affect the length of class periods, the number of periods, and the length of the school day. A decision in this area is going to affect teachers in their daily work. How can it be made without teachers?

The principal's administrative colleagues in his building will also have strong opinions on this subject. They will have to build the schedule, assign the teachers, arrange the classes, find classrooms, and try to give students the courses they request. Their responsibilities and the ease with which they can accomplish them will be dramatically affected by the kind of schedule used.

Students, of course, are also greatly affected by the school schedule. It tells them what time they must be in school, when their classes will meet, which teachers they will have—in which classrooms, when their "free" time will be, when they will have lunch and with whom, and what time their school day will end. Certainly, students will have to be consulted in any decision about the school schedule.

Because students are affected and will have preferences about their classes, their teachers, and the length of their day, parents are also concerned because they frequently evaluate their students' success in school by the schedule—starting and ending times, and the way time is used and supervised in the school. In addition, parents frequently get involved with the school's scheduling when they have family needs that require an early dismissal for part-time work, lessons, or baby sitting. Most assuredly, parents have a right to be involved in planning the schedule of the school day.

As if this involvement were not enough, the principal in a multiple-school district may also want to confer with his fellow principals in other schools to be sure he doesn't make decisions that are too much at variance with those schools. He can hardly expect to design a school schedule that requires his teachers and students to have a longer school day, to spend more time in class, or to have shorter (or longer) lunch periods. This district-wide coordination probably will involve the superintendent and his staff.

If the issues are controversial, the board of education may become involved as well, when those whose opinions have not been taken and followed appeal the principal's decision or process to the highest authority, the board of education. Boards of education will invariably expect the principal to accept full responsibility for making the schedule, but they can't ignore the complaints and appeals of those who feel the principal's decision has affected them adversely.

In addition, the principal will be bound by the constraints of school laws and the policies of the local district. These legal restraints may limit his latitude considerably. If he is to invite others to help him make the decision, he should make them fully aware of the parameters that limit the decision.

In the end, whose decision is it to change a school schedule? Should the principal hold open meetings and allow everyone to have a say? Should he form a committee of representatives from each group? Should he bring in consultants? Should he gather information, give all parties a fair hearing and then decide on his own? Should he hold a referendum, allowing every affected group an equal role in the decision? Should he negotiate the change with his teacher's union?

Hardly any of these alone, surely not all of them together, would be appropriate. It depends entirely on the nature of the decision and the processes that the principal feels will be helpful. It also depends on who has a legitimate right to participate, who has knowledge and expertise to contribute, and who will ultimately be affected.

Without question, decision making for the principal is not easy. Decisions that should be clear cut and simple sometimes take years in process. Faculties negotiate for channels to be used by their organizations to influence decision making. Students are trained by the schools to participate in the democratic process that leads to decisions that they will support. Parents' organizations are no longer "tea and cookies" social groups, whose purpose is to pitch in and support any school program whether they like it or believe in it or not. The Parent Teacher Association has changed its official posture from an organization to support and work for programs in the school to an activist organization to be involved in decision making. What is expected of the principal who feels the seat of his chair getting pretty hot at times? The principal needs a comprehensive job description which makes clear to everyone just what the limits and bounds of his authority are. This should be under constant review and should be noted by all participants at any time the principal is ready to involve any of his constiuent groups in the decision-making process.

The principal has to be process-oriented and skillful in discerning which groups need to be consulted, which should give advice, which should be informed (before or after), and which should participate fully to the extent of having their concurrence. Furthermore, he needs an unerring sense of when a decision should be made, when to delegate it to someone, when to delay, and when to have the constituent groups participate.

The wise principal, faced with these mounting expectations for involvement in and participation in decision making, should be candid with all he invites into the process. They should know precisely what their involvement is to be. If he knows beforehand irrevocably what his decision is going to be, he should not go through the pretense of seeking advice or asking for opinions or preferences. His credibility will suffer in that practice.

The principal is still the chief decision maker in his school. Decisions made by others in his organization— assistants, department heads, teachers, or students— will need his concurrence and his support. Few decisions will be made alone. In almost every instance, he will seek advice and consent from among his associates and his constituents, many of whom will doubtless be affected in some way by his decision.

13

A Problem Solver

EVERY SCHOOL HAS PROBLEMS—with facilities, with personnel, with finances, with program, with parents and students. Some problems grow out of conflict among groups or individuals. Opinions differ; groups compete for facilities or resources; students strive for the same position or honors; supervisors clash with subordinates; parents object to disciplinary actions.

Such conflicts and problems, if unresolved, invariably find their way to the principal's office which becomes the court of last resort.

Many of the administrative skills already described—and a few more—are needed by the principal in solving problems. No rules of thumb or convenient statements of policy can be applied in these instances. If it were so, someone would have applied them previously, and his involvement would not be necessary.

Because many problems are unprecedented and unique, the principal must call upon his skills as mediator, compromiser, and accommodator—particularly in conflict situations. Other problems may require extensive study and research, gathering of resources, and calling in consultants. All such techniques are used by principals. In such instances they must know what information is needed, who should be involved, and how long a problem should be allowed to "stew" before resolution. A cooling-off period is frequently helpful if emotions are involved. Snap judgments are not very useful and may be regretted soon afterward. Time is needed to solve many of the involved problems that rise through channels to the principal's level.

In the area of problem solving a principal can demonstrate his talents of educational statesmanship and creativity. The unique character of school problems calls for the principal's careful consideration and accurate perception of where solutions might lead. He must be able to predict accurately the consequences of his solution. Will it serve as a model for others to follow? What precedents are being established? Have the feelings and opinions of "the losers" been mollified? Will the solution at the principal's level only forward it to the superintendent's level? Does the solution settle the troublesome issue or just prolong or postpone the crisis?

A second phase of the NASSP study of the senior high school principalship deals with a group of 60 principals identified as exemplary and effective.[9] The study found them to be especially skillful problem solvers, both in their own eyes and the perceptions of the students, parents, and teachers, in their schools. These principals were good listeners. They seldom became defensive or emotional. They were able to take pressure and handle tension. They remained cool under fire. They were fair and reasonable, but firm. They displayed determination and perseverance.

The effective principals dealt with problems systematically and analytically, but also acknowledged that their own personal abilities as problem solvers and their own intuition played important roles in their success.

The principal must be a successful problem solver. There are no pat formulas or recipe books available for

---

9. Richard A. Gorton and Kenneth E. McIntyre, *The Senior High School Principalship. Volume Two: The Effective Principal* (Reston, Va.: National Association of Secondary School Principals, 1978).

easy reference. His skill will derive from his good judgment, his consideration of feelings and opinions, his sense of fairness, and his ability to take a position and persuade those affected to understand and support it. This requires good human relations skills, good sense, and courage of conviction.

14

The Master Schedule

No OTHER RESPONSIBILITY of the principal directly affects more people than the school schedule. The master schedule of classes is the school plan that brings students and teachers together in appropriate places for instruction and educational activity. Through the master schedule the goals of the school are met and the plans and aspirations of the individual students who follow the schedule every day are carried out.

School principals are always searching for better systems to schedule their school's educational programs. Someone is always coming up with a new scheduling idea which will revolutionize learning and solve the problems of education. There have been advocates of conventional schedules with 40, 45, 55, or 60-minute periods. There are 70-minute period schedules with days off for another class to be scheduled on the "diagonal" (the different days off). There are flexible schedules which use 15 or 20-minutes modules to vary the structure of the school day. Schedules are made with double-periods or half-periods—even one-and-a-half periods for certain kinds of classes. A few schools have even experimented with "daily demand" schedules where teachers are asked each day what time they want for their activities for the following day. Computers do this work, of course.

In all cases, they are still schedules, and once fixed, they are the plan by which the school operates for a school year. The schedule controls the beginning time and ending time for school as a whole and for every teacher and student. It places students with certain teachers. It gives everyone a certain time to eat, a time to study, a time to prepare, a time to relax, a time to move from one location to another. The schedule controls the activity of the school.

Master schedules in large schools are so complex and so many variables have to be controlled that computers are required to fit all the elements (time, students, teachers, rooms) together in an orderly, organized manner. Some schools allow students to make their own schedules, picking the period and the teacher — college style.

All this reveals that the principal's creativity and ingenuity in this area is a critical one. Probably in no other area of responsibility is he challenged so often and so vigorously as he tries to satisfy everyone's expectations for a "good" schedule. The master schedule has the potential of being the greatest "dis-satisfyer" in the school.

Teachers desire certain favorite classes to teach. They want classes assigned to certain rooms or in the same room. They do not want too many classes in succession without a break. They do not want low ability classes at the end of the day. And on and on.

Students want schedules that give them the subjects they have chosen. They prefer certain teachers. They do not care for too many classes in a row. Or they prefer all their classes in a row with no unscheduled time. They want early lunch—or late lunch. They want their day "compacted" so they can come late or leave early.

Parents want schedules that provide some convenience for their families also. They prefer an early —or a late one. They don't want too much unscheduled time that a student uses poorly and gets into "trouble." They want their children assigned to the "good" teachers, those that their older children have had and liked.

The principal, faced with these conflicting individual expectations and demands, just can't possibly win. His schedule has to be understood as a set of compromises which allocates resources in the most efficient way possible — time, spaces, teachers, materials — into a conflict-free, smoothly functioning, accommodating master schedule .

A good master schedule will be built upon these priorities — factors to be considered pretty much in this order:

- Students are scheduled into classes which they are required to take.
- Students are scheduled into classes they elect.
- Sufficient time is provided in the schedule for teachers and students to achieve the objectives of each course.
- An appropriately equipped classroom, resource area, laboratory, or activity area is available for each scheduled class.
- Students are not scheduled with long blocks of unscheduled time between classes.
- Proper supervision and controls are provided in the school and proper facilities are available for students when they are not scheduled in classes.
- All agreements on teacher assignments negotiated in board of education-teacher master contracts must be adhered to. These include number of students in each class, total number of students, number of lesson preparations, and number of consecutive teaching periods.
- Teachers are assigned in their areas of certification and expertise.

The aforementioned are imperatives, but the wise principal will try to satisfy these additional expectations:

- Teachers have their preferred classes.
- Students have their preferred teachers.
- Students have their school day adjusted for after-school student activities, out-of-school activities, and part-time work. (This is increasingly a parent expectation as well.)

- Certain extracurricular activities, meetings, rehearsals, and practices should be built into the participating students' school day.

Add to these priorities such issues as open lunch or open campus (students may leave school during lunch or unassigned periods), study halls, free movement in the building, and the common interferences with the school day like assemblies, field trips, and special programs — and the scheduling of the school day becomes an overwhelming dilemma for the principal and his associates who attempt to put all these puzzle pieces together.

Needless to say, principals who cannot work miracles (and none can) are not going to be able to generate a master schedule that satisfies everyone's expectations. Students and parents must recognize this and understand the intricacies of scheduling all the elements that make up a school.

15

A Disciplinarian

PRINCIPALS IN MANY SCHOOLS may not be directly responsible for the administration of discipline, but they won't be very far removed from those who are. Principals are directly involved in establishing the rules of behavior, the penalties to be applied, and the processes to be used. As the responsible head of the school, the principal cannot delegate this ultimate responsibility to anyone else.

The first line of discipline, of course, is maintained by teachers and other building supervisors as they deal with students in the classroom, in and about the school, and at school activities. In cases of more serious misbehavior or challenges to the teacher's authority, the principal or his delegate will step in. The delegate in larger schools will in all likelihood be an assistant principal or a dean of discipline. In all cases the principal's influence will be felt, his authority always present.

Principals have learned that their authority in the area of student discipline is not absolute. Primarily because of court decisions during the 1960s and 1970s, schools have had to exercise greater discretion in penalizing students, particularly when the penalties deny students their right to an education (suspension or expulsion). In many states in years past, the principal had the final authority to expel a student from school. There was no requirement for any due process, hearings, testimony, or appeal. The student was at the absolute mercy of the principal.

Principals no longer have that authority. In most states, before a student can be expelled, the principal must be able to document the misbehavior (with dates, names, and descriptions of events), must be able to show all the efforts the school has made to provide educational alternatives for the student, must show how the student and his family had been advised and warned of eventual consequences, and finally must put his case before a hearing officer appointed by the board of education. The hearing may involve such court proceedings as sworn-in witnesses, defense attorneys, cross-examination, marked and numbered exhibits, character witnesses, and court reporters to record the entire process. The final authority for expulsion from school rests with the board of education, and in states like Illinois this exclusion can be only for the current school term.

There are other limitations on the disciplinary authority of the principal. Some are spelled out in law, some are established through the precedent of court decisions. Schools no longer can make arbitrary rules about student dress, length of hair, freedom of expression, and searches of students' person or possessions (even lockers). Accusations of wrongdoing, particularly in serious cases, must be made with utmost care.

The Constitution protects students' rights in school just as it protects all citizens' rights in society at large. This may not mean the same kind of formality as *Miranda* warnings and prohibitions against search and seizure, but it can and should mean limits on cruel and unusual means of punishment. Corporal punishment is definitely used less in schools today. Many districts prohibit it. When it is used, it is administered under carefully controlled circumstances, with adult witnesses.

In spite of these limitations and restrictions, principals are expected to maintain an orderly, controlled atmosphere where learning can take place. Limits on disruptive behavior are necessary. The wise principal establishes these limits through some democratic process that will involve students, parents, and faculty members.

Most schools do have codes of behavior, published in student guidebooks. These codes cover rules for attendance, tardiness, smoking, social behavior, and use of facilities and campus. Serious misbehavior such as fighting, stealing, vandalism, drug or alcohol use, firearms, gross disobedience, or insubordination are also included.

Those administering discipline should have considerable discretion in meting out punishment. The penalty itself is not so important as it is for the action to be prompt, fair, reasonable, and certain. Today's students have a highly developed sense of fairness and they know their rights. They can accept discipline when they know that it is necessary for the orderly conduct of school, when they have had something to say about the rules, when the rules are well-known to everyone (that is, published), and when they are administered equitably to everyone.

If the principal has delegated very much of his authority and responsibility for discipline to subordinates, when will he personally intercede and accept final responsibility? The principal will be involved any time there is serious misbehavior such as group activity (riots), collective insubordination, drug activity, challenges to authority or school policy, assaults against adult personnel, law violations involving police. In all cases he will be directly involved in recommendations to expel students from school.

Rules of behavior should be based on a philosophy of discipline that is consistent with community standards for courtesy, respect, morality, and general decorum. The limits should not be arbitrary and inflexible, but should be clearly understood to be there for a reason. Young people need limits on their behavior. Most of them expect limits. Most of them *want* limits. Many will be confused and insecure if adults do not set limits for them.

This may mean curfews, driving and parking regulations, requirements for attendance, and various prohibitions. Adolescents and preadolescents can be expected to protest and rebel against such "limits on their freedom" or "limitations of their rights," but they will be disappointed in parents, teachers, and principals if they do not provide this supervision and control. If adults care for and love their children, they will provide discipline.

The laws and court decisions cannot be used as an excuse for the principal to abdicate his responsibility for discipline. Rules and procedures should stand the test of reasonableness. The question should be, "What would a reasonable parent do in this instance?" Although the rule of *in loco parentis* has been challenged and eroded to a degree, school teachers and principals are still responsible for discipline of children while the child is at school. Parents should be able to expect that reasonable standards of courtesy, morals, and respect for authority will be enforced in the school. The principal is the person most directly responsible for this supervision of students at school.

16

Setting Goals

A MAJOR RESPONSIBILITY of principals is keeping their schools goal-oriented and working toward accepted educational goals. No other person in the school has such overall responsibility.

Custodians see the school as a building in need of cleaning and repair. Cooks see little besides hungry students. Secretaries confront voluminious clerical work, typing, sorting, filing, and distributing. Even teachers become so engrossed in teaching their favorite concepts and content that they lose sight of why these concepts or content are taught. Administrators, too, sometimes give the impression that order and discipline in the school are paramount, that smoothness of operation is the ultimate goal.

Employees in the schools need to be reminded regularly that schools are not for them and their livelihood; rather, that schools are to educate children. The principal, as the educational leader and person held directly responsible at the building level, helps everyone keep his attention and effort directed at the goals of the school. He is watchful and sensitive for signs that indicate the machinery and the workers are becoming more important than the product.

This means that each school should have clearly identified, easily understood, educational goals. Such goal statements are common in every local school district.

Unfortunately, they are too often devised through elaborate processes of community involvement, then put on the shelf and forgotten.

Adoption of such philosophical statements of a school's purpose is the responsibility of the board of education, representing the community. The statements should clearly reflect the character of the community and its values. Educational goals should have the endorsement of the citizenry who pay the cost. The professional educators may have an advisory role, but they cannot and should not set the goals. The most enlightened communities over the country have used extensive communication networks to ensure that citizens participate in determining what the schools should be teaching their children.

Purposes of education seldom are very controversial. National commissions and even presidential task forces have established what most everyone accepts as basic goals for education. They are frequently as high sounding and idealistic as the famous Seven Cardinal Principles, articulated in 1918 and improved on very little since then:

1. Health
2. Command of fundamental processes
3. Worthy home membership
4. Vocation
5. Citizenship
6. Worthy use of leisure
7. Ethical character.

The principal in each school, as the responsible curriculum planner, utilizes the expertise of his faculty to devise educational experiences that will accomplish the goals agreed upon. The courses offered should contribute directly to the overall district philosophy. Teachers should share with their students what these course objectives are and how they will achieve them. The good teacher also shares with students the plan for evaluation of the learning — before the teaching begins. All of this goal setting and planning in the school is carried out under the principal's direction.

In some schools, principals may find resistance to writing of course objectives and planning for evaluation. Teachers want to be trusted to use their professional training and their expertise to provide instruction without much administrative supervision. Principals will need to remind teachers that this is a time for strictest accountability, that parents and taxpayers have lost much of their confidence in what schools have been accomplishing with their children and are demanding that schools get better results.

The principal cannot ignore the community's interests.

17

An Influential Position

A CANDIDATE FOR THE PRINCIPALSHIP recently recounted how a committee of teachers involved by the superintendent in the selection process confronted him with the question: "Why do we need a principal? Our present principal has been away from the school because of illness and we have gotten along just fine. The department chairpersons are running the school."

Although the question was intended to challenge the candidate and get him to express his views on what a principal should do, the question was not a frivolous one. Teachers particularly, reinforced by the belief that their professional organization or union should be making decisions the principal makes, question the need to have administrators in their schools. In the particular school where this provocative question was posed to the candidate, teachers had to acknowledge that there was a considerable vacuum in leadership and supervision in their school. Student discipline was out of hand. Teachers were unsupervised and had received no formal evaluation for some time. The master schedule of classes, with teacher assignments, had not been made. There was no program or plan for curriculum development and assessment.

In short, without leadership from the principal, everyone appeared to be on his own, doing what he pleased. The conditions in the school were chaotic and disorganized.

Some people seriously advocate administration by committee. Particularly in schools with highly trained, professional employees, the employee group believes that their collective expertise could supplant the role of a single administrator, the principal. School boards, since the advent of collective bargaining, have actually had this proposal presented by teachers at the bargaining table. No boards of education, to the author's knowledge, have ever acceded to this appeal. Legally, they would be abdicating their own responsibility and authority.

Why do schools need administrators (principals)? First and foremost is the legal responsibility of boards of education to establish philosophy and objectives for their schools, to create policies for their implementation, and to employ executive officers (superintendents), and administrators (assistant superintendents, principals, assistant principals, and supervisors) to carry out their policies.

Schools are not autonomous entities. Teachers and administrators are not independent entrepreneurs. They are all regulated by state school codes and local board of education policies. Boards levy taxes, establish budgets, allocate resources, approve staffing, employ personnel, set goals, approve curriculum, and create policies for the conduct of education in the schools. No superintendent, principal, or committee of teachers has the legal authority to make any of those decisions.

In addition to the legal need to have administrators in the schools to carry out board of education mandates, the schools, like any other large, complex organizations, need someone to administer them. Melton and Stanavage expressed it well. [10]

> The secondary school, like any other corporate endeavor, requires conscious and constant administration. No school can realize its purposes without

---

10. George E. Melton and John Stanavage "Job Specifications for "Principals," *The Principalship* (Washington, D.C.: National Association of Secondary School Principals, 1970).

someone assuming the responsibility of helping the many persons involved clarify objectives, identify progress. Moreover, if utter chaos is to be avoided, someone must integrate into a meaningful whole the discrete, disparate efforts of those who, taken together, constitute the school. It is, of course, the principal who is charged with this vital leadership role.

The principalship has been and promises to continue to be one of the critically influential positions of leadership in American education. The 20,000 secondary school principals throughout the nation have demonstrated their ability and their willingness to furnish this leadership for the benefit of junior and senior high school youth in the years ahead.

Principals who are prepared thoroughly and who have developed leadership and management skills as decribed in this monograph can and will provide the leadership, supervision, and evaluation, that students, parents, and lay persons expect in good secondary schools throughout the nation.

Appendix

TIME LOG OF SENIOR HIGH SCHOOL PRINCIPAL

7:35 a.m. Arrived at school. Picked up mail and communications. Unlocked desk.

7:36 a.m. Looked for dean who wasn't in yet. Left word for him to see me.

7:38 a.m. Looked at mail—Heart Association wanting to promote a "Heart Day." Worked at desk, proofread two teacher evaluations.

7:47 a.m. Secretary came in. Gave her evaluations of teachers for retyping.

7:49 a.m. Checked with substitute clerk for absentees and late-comers (exceptionally foggy morning).

7:50 a.m. Spoke briefly with arriving English teacher abut his spelling bee and award certificates I had signed.

7:52 a.m. Called five administrative offices, suggesting they check classrooms for possible late teachers.

7:54 a.m. Gave secretary instructions on duplicating and distribution of material on change in graduation requirement.

7:55 a.m. Saw dean about student who had called after school yesterday—threatened and beaten up by other students getting off bus.

7:58 a.m.	On way to staffing, stopped at attendance office to visit with parent who was in about son not doing well in school.
8:00 a.m.	Joined staffing with social worker, psychologist, counselor, therapist, parent, and student who had been removed from all classes for truancy.
9:10 a.m.	Left staffing to look for student who had been told to wait in outer office but had wandered off.
9:15 a.m.	Found student in hall, returned to staffing.
9:30 a.m.	Left staffing to keep appointment with candidate for maintenance job.
9:31 a.m.	While waiting for building and grounds director to arrive, gave secretary instructions for cover and illustrations for the open house printed program.
9:33 a.m.	While waiting read: Note from student needing early release. Bulletin from National Federation of Athletic Associations on college recruiting of high school athletes. Note from teacher upset over misbehavior in previous day's home room program. Staff absentee report for the day.
9:36 a.m.	Went to outer office to greet candidate and explain why we were waiting.
9:37 a.m.	Called building and grounds director and learned he wasn't coming over.
9:39 a.m.	Interviewed maintenance supervisor candidate.
10:00 a.m.	Took call from registrar—to be returned.
10:07 a.m.	Completed interview.
10:08 a.m.	Saw teacher who had pictures from German exchange program.
10:09 a.m.	Called for building and grounds director—busy.
10:10 a.m.	Returned call to registrar about purging of

	records of a dropout.
10:11 a.m.	Called building and grounds director to discuss maintenance candidate.
10:14 a.m.	Returned call to personnel director about administrator's inservice program next week Agreed to make a presentation.
10:22 a.m.	Read:
	Two suspension notices.
	Plans of special programs coming up.
10:25 a.m.	Saw special programs coordinator in outer office. Approved her plans and discussed possible appearance of Navy Band in February.
10:27 a.m.	Saw dean to learn what he had done about yesterday's incident.
10:30 a.m.	Left for cafeteria—talked with counselor in hall about Guidance Information Service (computer service for college selection).
10:31 a.m.	Stopped by to see psychologist to hear outcome of staffing meeting.
10:36 a.m.	Stopped by health center to give nurses information from Heart Association about "Heart Day."
	Talked with nurse about her program at a PTSA meeting the previous day.
10:37 a.m.	Stopped in Audiovisual Center to ask director to prepare transparencies I had given him for inservice program.
10:40 a.m.	Stopped by athletic director's office to relate comments by parents about physical education that had come up at the PTSA meeting.
10:45 a.m.	Checked on the room where I was to have lunch with two students. Visited with a student congress representative who was there.
10:46 a.m.	Looked in on yearbook photographer who was waiting for students to come in for underclass pictures.
	Visited with student who had performed with

choir previous day when students had misbehaved.

10:49 a.m.   Walked down to maintenance office to tell men about holes broken in wall of the student council office.

10:52 a.m.   Stayed around student cafeteria. Spoke with teacher who was in school exchange.

10:54 a.m.   Stopped in faculty lounge to visit with three soccer coaches who were concerned about new play-off rules that eliminated our team.

10:57 a.m.   Picked up lunch and went to council office to meet students.

11:00 a.m.   Lunched with two students.

11:30 a.m.   Stopped and visited with a few students in the cafeteria.

11:35 a.m.   Returned to the office. On the way, stopped to visit with CVE teacher about cosmetology program and a student in the program.

11:38 a.m.   Visited with workmen installing new air conditioning units in office area.

11:40 a.m.   Made four telephone calls. No answer on two of them.

11:47 a.m.   Returned call from fellow principal, discussed graduation requirement proposal.

11:48 a.m.   Answered note from teacher.

11:50 a.m.   Reviewed minutes of previous day's principal's advisory committee meeting (principal is chairman and secretary).

11:51 a.m.   Read note from teacher about a student's early release.

11:52 a.m.   Looked up material needed for next day's athletic conference meeting.

11:58 a.m.   Read communications:
Memo regarding special education student.
Note from teacher about conduct in homeroom.
Memo from special program coordinator about upcoming program.

Board of Education summary.

November homeroom calendar.

12:07 p.m. Called in building manager to discuss his problems that students had brought up in advisory meeting.

12:22 p.m. Saw student who was upset with dean's handling of his absence.

12:28 p.m. Took call from a mother who didn't want her daughter to drop out of school.

12:30 p.m. Met with two teachers to make plans for disseminating information to faculty, parent, and student groups on graduation requirement change.

1:08 p.m. Completed conference.

Instructed secretary to prepare materials.

1:09 p.m. The day's mail—read, routed, and filed.

1:12 p.m. Made two calls. No answer for either.

1:13 p.m. Called PTSA president. No answer.

1:15 p.m. Wrote note to superintendent to accompany graduation requirement proposals.

1:20 p.m. Saw student council representative about floor hockey marathon project.

1:23 p.m. Gave dictation to secretary:

Memo to administrators and faculty inservice committee about faculty meeting date.

Petition form for faculty for graduation requirement proposal.

Letter to parents for principal's coffee next month.

Welcome letter to parents for the open house program.

Faculty bulletin for next day.

1:46 p.m. Took call from district administrator's secretary.

1:48 p.m. Received note from teacher on a student's early release.

Gave secretary several instructions.

1:54 p.m. Called PTSA president. No answer.

1:55 p.m.	Called assistant administrator about our school hosting a student congress (forensic event).
1:56 p.m.	Went to student services office to review memo to teachers responsible for the previous day's homeroom.
2:02 p.m.	Walked out to smoking area. Admonished a student athlete for being there.
2:11 p.m.	Called both fellow principals, neither in, left word to call.
2:14 p.m.	Called administrator at sister school who was on graduation requirements committee.
2:15 p.m.	Conferred with secretary about dictation.
2:15 p.m.	Called personnel office about tuition scholarships from college whose student teachers we help train.
2:18 p.m.	Read more communications: Five suspension notices. Note from teacher on the early release of student. Daily bulletin.
2:20 p.m.	Wrote note to student services director about homeroom programs for November.
2:21 p.m.	Read bulletin from National Federation of Activities Associations.
2:27 p.m.	Studied six-week grade distributions—computer printout.
2:33 p.m.	Answered question for student reporter about early dismissal on open house day.
2:34 p.m.	Continued study of grade distributions. Made summary table of withdraw-passing and withdraw-failing grades.
2:42 p.m.	Read confirmation of an order to change telephone service.
2:44 p.m.	Read principals' association newsletter.
2:48 p.m.	Took return call from fellow principal. Discussed institute day program.

	Arrangements for next day's league meeting. Graduation requirements proposal strategy.
2:50 p.m.	Received material from superintendent to be distributed to faculty—read material and gave secretary instructions for distribution.
3:00 p.m.	Saw newspaper adviser about a story on graduation requirement proposal
3:02 p.m.	Returned to reading principals' newsletter.
3:05 p.m.	Called fellow principal about ride to league meeting next day.
3:07 p.m.	Called PTSA president. No answer.
3:08 p.m.	Reviewed agenda for league meeting—got material together.
3:10 p.m.	Took call from athletic director about cuts in capital equipment budget.
3:12 p.m.	Read a teacher evaluation.
3:15 p.m.	School is out.
3:18 p.m.	Went into hall—watched students and teachers leave.
3:22 p.m.	Helped a student look for a lost jacket.
3:25 p.m.	Back in office, went over open house program with secretary.
3:30 p.m.	Called assistant administrator. No answer. Left word to call.
3:33 p.m.	Called PTSA president. Busy this time.
3:37 p.m.	Studied curriculum council's grade weighting system.
3:45 p.m.	Called PTSA president—discussed agenda for next week's board meeting.
3:50 p.m.	Left school for a personal appointment.